I0199412

Where Does Time Go?
by Dave E. Keliher
Illustrations by
Erika L. Chan

Text copyright ©2016 Free The Pig (dave keliher)

Illustration copyright ©2016 Erika L. Chan

All rights reserved.

Published by Free The Pig

ISBN 978-0-9970818-4-8

Printed in the United States of America

For Patricia "Mom" Keliher
and Joyce Wright and Kat and YOU!
(P.S. and a special thank you to
Joe Ryan and his memoir writing class
(at Los Angeles City College) who got things rolling.
And a BIG thank you to Erika L. Chan for
bringing my story to life!)

When I was a young boy long, long ago, I asked many questions as children are naturally apt to do. But the question that arose on this particular day was not mine at first. It came about in this way.

One Thanksgiving Day, our family gathered together to give thanks for all the good things we had.

After the meal, the grown-ups sat in the living room talking about important things like hibachi barbeques and lava lamps while we played Red Rover, Red Rover outside.

I had entered the house to use the bathroom when I overheard my Aunt Sharon ask, "Where does the time go?"

I really wanted to stay and hear the reply, but I had other business to attend to and couldn't wait.

When I returned to the living room, I hoped to hear the answer to the question asked moments before.

I hung around the passageway but the conversation had turned to the television where the Detroit Lions' defense was upsetting my father considerably.

That night, as I lay in bed, I could not stop thinking about *time*. I looked at the clock and watched the second hand go 'round and 'round.

I got up and turned back the clock and it seemed, as best I could tell in the darkness illuminated softly by the clock, that I had set time back. There was no indication otherwise. So I set it back some more. And I continued to do this for quite some time until I was awakened by my mom calling me to get up and go help my father rake the leaves.

I looked at the clock. It was only 4:00 a.m. Why was she waking me up at 4:00 a.m.? I went downstairs to the kitchen and asked,

"Why do I have to get up so early?"

"What are you talking about?" she asked. "It's eight-thirty. You've overslept as it is."

"But my clock says it's only four."

"Your clock must be in need of repair. Now get some breakfast and go outside and help your father with the leaves."

"Okay," I said. And then I asked, "Can you stop time? I've heard of time standing still."

"Time stands still for no one," she said.

"No one? Not even you?"

"Not a soul. Especially not me."

That was news to me. I ate my breakfast and went out to do my chores. As I raked the leaves with my pop I couldn't stop thinking about time. I asked, "Who is Father Time?"

"He's Mother Nature's husband."

"Oh. Where do they live?" I asked.

"Vermont."

I stopped raking the leaves and my jaw dropped. I was astounded to hear such a thing. "Father Time and Mother Nature live in Vermont?"

"Yes, at least in the summertime. In the winter they go to Miami."

"Why Miami?"

"The winters are too hard on them. They're very old, you know."

"But how can—"

"Keep raking," he said.

I didn't finish my sentence because in my head my brain was spinning a gazillion miles an hour as I was thinking,

"How can winters be hard on Mother Nature? Isn't winter one of Mother Nature's coats—similar to the fall coat but heavier and with much less color? I mean, weren't they the same thing?"

Jumpin' Jehosaphat! This was something I had to tell my friend Luther.

When I finished raking the leaves, I went over to Luther's house where my other friend Teresa had just arrived.

"Hey," I said, "guess what! Mother Nature lives with Father Time in Vermont!"

"What the heck are you talking about?" asked Luther. He was always skeptical.

I repeated, "Mother Nature lives with Father Time in Vermont!"

"Who told you that?" asked Teresa.

"My pop," I said.

"Your pop also told you we have 'nuf nuclear weapons to blow up the world a thousand times and we know that's stupid because why would anyone wanna do that?" said Luther.

"Yeah," said Teresa, "if you blow it up once you got nothin' to blow up after that. Be a big waste."

I decided not to tell them about Mother Nature and Father Time going to Florida in the winter. They would just hassle me and I didn't feel like being hassled.

That night, while lying in bed, I was still wondering about the time thing. So I decided to go ask my mom. She had better answers than Pop. (Years later I found out she made up a lot of the answers, too. I guess that's why they got along so swell. But that's okay. At least she listened to me.)

"Mom," I asked the next day, "where does time go?"

She was standing in the kitchen peeling potatoes. I think she actually welcomed the break. She put down the paring knife and gestured for me to sit at the table.

She replied, "Long ago, I asked the same question of my mom, your Grandma Carmichael. And she told me that when we are born into this world, we are given many gifts. But the most precious gift of all was time."

"How much time do we get?" I asked.

"Some of us are given a day, others a year or twenty and still others a hundred or more."

"But how come we don't all get the same amount?" I asked.

"No one really knows. But it's not how much you get but what you do with the time you have. There are some who live more fully in ten years than those who live to one hundred. We shouldn't waste the time we have because we don't know if tomorrow will bring us any more."

"You mean I may not have any more time?" If that was true I sure wasn't going to sleep tonight!

"Don't worry. You only have so much time to spend and if you spend it on worry, you won't get your money's worth."

"Is that what they mean when they say 'time is money'?"

"Time is not necessarily money itself. But you can look at time as something to be spent. And you don't want to spend it just anywhere. The real difference between time and money is you can always get more money, but you can never get more time."

"If I don't know how much time I have left, can I have the television put back into my room? I'd like to spend some time with it before I go."

"I don't think that's the best use of your time."

That was debatable but I decided not to argue the point. I asked, "But where does time go when the day is over?"

"Time goes away to the Land of Memories where it sits by the sea and waits for the rest of your time to come. And when all the time you have has passed, you will follow and sit by the sea with all your memories and your friends and your loves and your losses."

"How long will I stay there?"

"Forever. Once you arrive time ceases to be. In the Land of Memories, time is timeless."

"Will you be there?"

"Yes, I will because I love you very much. So much of my time has been spent dreaming about having a child like you to love and care for. Much of our time will be spent together. And for years to come, I will spend my time doing what I can to make you happy and keep you safe."

That was good news to me. I liked being happy and safe.

"Where does your time go?" I asked.

"My time also goes to the sea where it will sit and wait for me. And when the time comes for me to go, I will be there and you will continue to spend your time here."

"Does time really heal all wounds?" I asked.

"Time is a wonderful medicine and it will cure all that troubles us. It is important to let time heal you while you still have time left to spend here. But some people resist and hold on to their troubles and refuse to let time make them better. In the end, we all go to the sea where we eventually find peace."

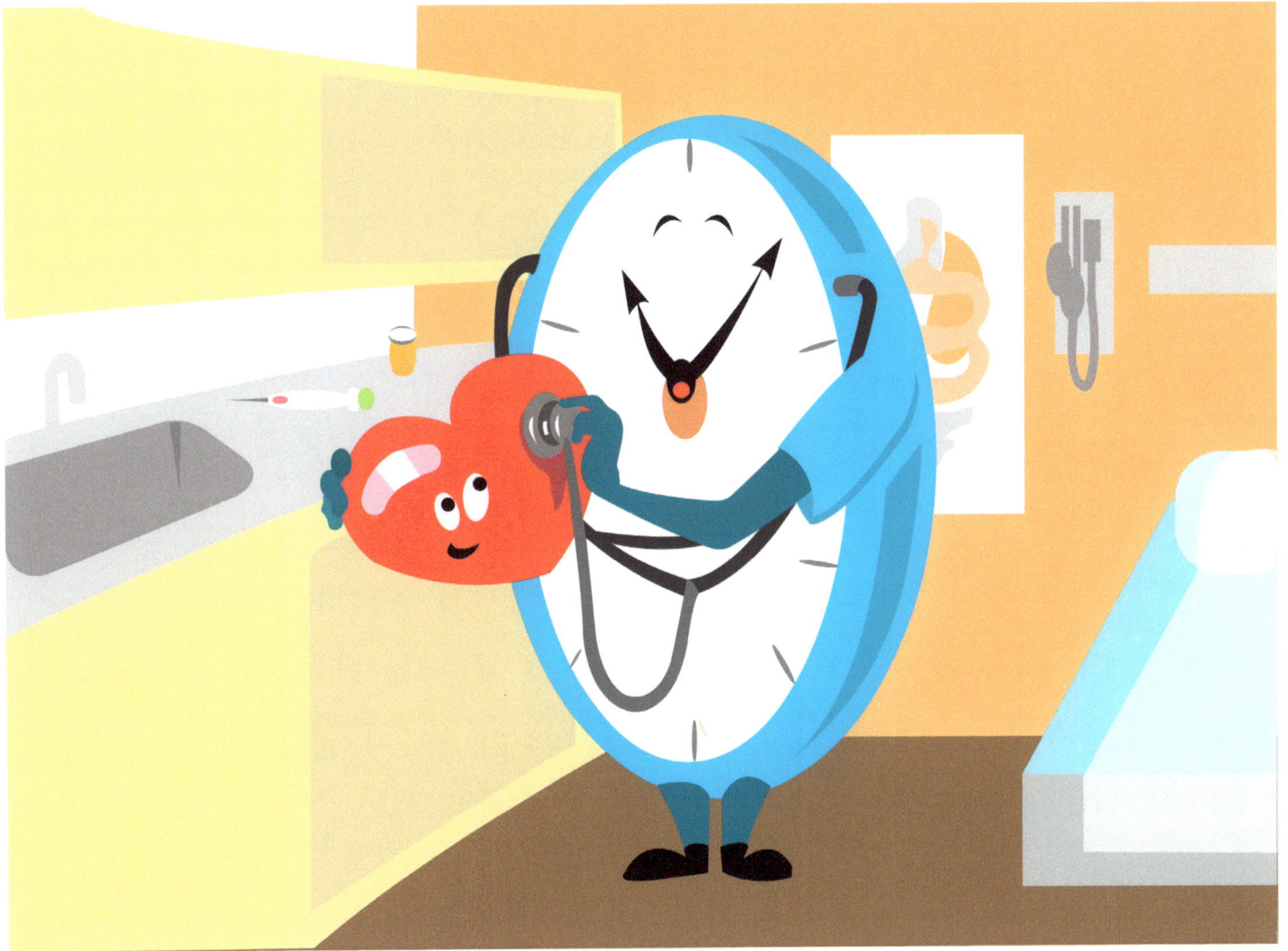

"How does time get to the sea?"

"You've heard the expression 'time flies', haven't you?" she asked.

"Oh, yes. Of course. It flies!" I said.

I thought for a moment and then asked, "But doesn't it fly only when we're having fun?"

"No. It flies all the time, all around us. Time is flying right now. It's hard for you to see at your age. And though your eyesight fades as you grow older, there are other things you can see much more clearly. Time flying is one."

"What's another?"

"Mistakes we have made." (Suddenly a look of sadness washed over her face.)

"What mistakes have you made?" I asked. (I didn't know mothers could make mistakes.)

The sad look passed as quickly and quietly as it had come.

"We all make mistakes. We should not be afraid to make mistakes. We should only fear not taking chances."

"Oh."

She looked at her hands.

She looked at the potatoes to be peeled.

She looked at me and put her hands out and brought me to her. She held me and stroked my hair and kissed my head and said,

"I love you very much. Now go outside and spend your time being happy."

I stood and as we parted I thought I saw time fly. This moment in time that we just shared had left and was gone, on its way to the sea, where it was to wait for her, was to wait for me.

I went outside. I decided not to tell Luther or Teresa what my mom had told me. Even though I wasn't all that sure what she said was true, I wanted to believe it was so. And I knew believing can make some things real. A rabbit taught me that.

But most important of all, now that I've grown up, I have remembered that the time we have is a precious gift and I have tried to spend it wisely and with care. Thank you, dear Mother, for that.

This was written for my mother, Patricia Ann, whom I do love with all my heart.

There are many reasons I wrote this for her.

For one, she cared for me—and did her darnedest to raise me to adulthood in the best way she could. And I do say she did a wonderful job.

Near the top of the list I'd like to add two more. One, she potty-trained me and this is very important if you plan to work outside the household.

And two, she taught me to read. I was not always a good reader. In the first grade, we had different reading groups. There were the Jaguars, who were fast and comprehended much. And there were the Elephants, who were not particularly fast but could at least remember what they had read. And then there was the third group, the Sloths, of which I was one. Sloths not only read slowly but spent a lot of time sleeping at their desks. I had a good reason for sleeping at my desk. I used to stay up late at night and watch Laurel & Hardy and Buster Keaton movies, which I thought were particularly funny.

When my parents found out I was a Sloth, they removed the television from my room and then my mom sat me down and began to read with me. (My Dad would have helped but he was usually busy polishing his shoes and preparing his lunch for work the next day. This took up a considerable amount of his time.)

The book my mom selected to read with me was *Green Eggs and Ham* by Dr. Seuss. I believed it won the Nobel Peace Prize for Literature, which is why my mom chose it. She knew how important it was.

For those of you who have not had the pleasure of reading it, I will say in brief, that it is a tale of conflict and woe that befalls a strange creature who is pursued mercilessly, à la Jean Valjean in *Les Misérables*, wherein the antagonist insists the protagonist eat a plate full of moldy and rotting green eggs (pilfered from some endangered species of bird) and ham (which is a euphemism for pig parts). Now everyone knows or should know that pigs are as smart as dogs and you wouldn't eat your dog, would you? I should think not.

It was reading this tome that ignited a spark in me for the written word and propelled me from Sloth to Jaguar. For two score and many more years, my mom, who was also a librarian, continued to feed the fire by bringing home wonderful books. And she still does to this day. What a mom!

And it is for these reasons mentioned (and many others not mentioned) that I tell this tale as it was told to me so long ago.

And that is how this all began.

–Dave "the middle son" Keliher

Erika L. Chan

Erika is an illustrator who was born in southern California. Much of her inspiration is derived from her love for animals, her travels and childhood memories. She enjoys questioning the mysteries and magic of our world and beyond and hopes her drawings, paintings and teachings will inspire and bring joy to people. Erika met Dave while she was working in Education at the Los Angles Zoo. She currently resides in San Francisco as a dog walker and dog trainer by day and an artist by night.

www.erikalchan.com

www.ingramcontent.com/pod-product-compliance
Lightning Source LLC
Chambersburg PA
CBHW042023090426

42811CB00016B/1713